What Living Things Need

Air

Vic Parker

Heinemann Library
Chicago, Illinois

Customer Service 888-454-2279

Visit our website at www.heinemannraintree.com

Printed and bound in China by South China Printing Company Limited
Photo research by Ruth Blair and Andrea Sadler

10 09 08 07 06
10 9 8 7 6 5 4 3 2 1

Library of Congress Cataloging-in-Publication Data

Parker, Victoria.
   Air / Vic Parker.
       p. cm. -- (What living things need)
Includes bibliographical references and index.
ISBN 1-4034-7882-1 (library binding-hardcover : alk. paper) -- ISBN 1-4034-7888-0 (pbk. : alk. paper)
1. Respiration--Juvenile literature. 2. Respiratory organs--Juvenile literature. 3. Air--Juvenile literature. I. Title. II. Series.
   QP121.P28 2007
   612.2--dc22
                                              2005025125

Acknowledgments
The author and publishers are grateful to the following for permission to reproduce copyright material: Corbis pp. **6**, **7**, **8**, **14** (John Conrad), back cover (kite); FLPA p. **4** (David Hosking); FLPA (Minden Pictures) pp. **15**, **16**, **23** (insects); Getty Images p. **5**; Getty Images (Digital Vision) pp. **12**, **19**, **23** (gills); Getty Images (Photodisc) pp. **11**, **17**, **23** (breathe), back cover (butterfly); Getty Images (Stone) pp. **13**, **23** (oxygen); Getty Images (Taxi) pp. **22**, **23** (air tank); NHPA (Martin Harvey) p. **21**; Photofusion p. **10** (Paul Baldesere), **20** (J. Chapman); TopFoto pp. **9** (Ellen B Senisi, The Image Works), **18** (Avampini, V&W, The Image Works).

Cover photograph reproduced with permission of Alamy.

Every effort has been made to contact copyright holders of any material reproduced in this book. Any omissions will be rectified in subsequent printings if notice is given to the publisher.

Many thanks to the teachers, library media specialists, reading instructors, and educational consultants who have helped develop the Read and Learn/Lee y aprende brand.

Contents

Some words are shown in bold, **like this**. You can find them in the picture glossary on page 23.

What Is a Living Thing?

Living things are things that grow.

People, animals, and plants are living things.

Which things in this picture are living and which are not?

What Is Air?

Air is all
around us.

But you cannot
see, smell, or
taste air.

You can feel air moving when you are on a swing.

Do We Need Air?

We need air to talk, think, and move.

We need air to grow.

How Does Air Get Inside Us?

You take air into your body through your nose and mouth.

This is called breathing.

You **breathe** air out again that way, too.

Do We Need Air All of the Time?

We need air all of the time.

We **breathe** air without thinking about it.

Air has **oxygen** in it. You cannot live without oxygen for long.

Hold your breath and see.

Do Animals Need Air?

All living things need air.

Many animals **breathe** through their nose and mouth, like we do.

beak

Do you know the name for
a bird's mouth?

Do All Animals Breathe Like Us?

Not all animals **breathe** like us.

Insects have mouths, but they use them just for eating.

Insects do not have noses.

They breathe through tiny holes in their bodies.

Can Animals Breathe Underwater?

blow hole

Some animals need to hold their breath when they go underwater.

This whale is coming up for air.

gills

Fish can **breathe** underwater.

They get **oxygen** from the water.

Fish breathe through openings
called **gills**.

How Do Plants Breathe?

Plants do not **breathe** like people.

They take in air through tiny holes in their leaves.

All plants take in air.

Little flowers take in air.
So do big, tall trees.

Can You Guess?

air tank

Can you guess how this person is breathing underwater?

He is using an **air tank**.

Glossary

 air tank a metal box filled with air with a tube to your mouth, so you can breathe underwater

 **breathe** pull air into and out of the body

 gills openings in a fish's body where air from the water goes in and out

 **insects** animals with six legs, such as beetles

 **oxygen** part of air

Index

Note to Parents and Teachers

Reading nonfiction texts for information is an important part of a child's literacy development. Readers can be encouraged to ask simple questions and then use the text to find the answers. Most chapters in this book begin with a question. Read the questions together. Look at the pictures. Talk about what the answer might be. Then read the text to find out if your predictions were correct. To develop readers' enquiry skills, encourage them to think of other questions they might ask about the topic. Discuss where you could find the answers. Assist children in using the contents page, picture glossary, and index to practise research skills and new vocabulary.